KETO DIET

COOKBOOK

A Complete List Of What To Eat And Avoid, Plus 7day Sample Menu And 20 Keto Diet Dinners You Can Make Early

Dr. Linda Shelton

TABLE OF CONTENTS

INTRODUCTION

CHAPTER ONE

A Total Food Manual for Follow

CHAPTER TWO

A Nitty-gritty Ketogenic Diet Food Rundown to Follow

CHAPTER THREE

7-Day Test Menu for the Keto Diet

CHAPTER FOUR

20 Keto Diet Dinners You Can Make Early

CHAPTER FIVE

CONCLUSION

INTRODUCTION

You'll need to cut your carbs on the keto diet, focusing on protein, non-starchy veggies, and solid fats.

In case you're hoping to get a kick off on your wellbeing and wellness objectives this year, you might be contemplating attempting the ketogenic diet. Possibly you've heard the expression previously — it's a colossal eating routine popular expression — yet aren't sure what it implies. Here's a preliminary: The ketogenic diet is an eating plan that drives your body into ketosis. In this state, the body utilizes fat as an essential fuel source (rather than starches).

At the point when you're eating the food varieties that get you there (additional on that in a moment), your body can enter a condition of ketosis in one to three days. Most of the calories you devour from the eating regimen come from fat, with a little protein and almost no sugars. Ketosis additionally occurs on the off chance that you eat an extremely low-calorie diet — think specialist administered, medicinally prescribed eating regimens of 600 to 800 all out calories each day.

Advantages and Dangers of the Eating regimen That Amateurs Need to Know

Before you take a plunge, it's vital to know the potential advantages and dangers of keto.

Exploration backs up endeavour a ketogenic diet in three conditions: to help treatment of epilepsy, to assist with overseeing type 2 diabetes, and help weight reduction and the last two purposes need more examinations. As far as diabetes, there is some encouraging exploration showing that the ketogenic diet may improve glycemic control. It's anything but a decrease in A1C — a critical test for diabetes that actions an individual's normal glucose command more than a few months — something that may assist you with lessening prescription use.

However, for individuals with diabetes, one major concern is you're eating a ton of fat on keto, and that fat might be immersed, which is undesirable when eaten in abundance. (The a lot higher absolute fat admission is likewise a test among keto novices.)

Since individuals with type 2 diabetes are at expanded danger for cardiovascular infection, there's a particular worry that the immersed fat in the eating routine may drive up LDL, or "awful," cholesterol levels, and further increment the chances of heart issues. On the off chance that you have type 2 diabetes, converse with your primary care physician before endeavouring a ketogenic diet. She

may suggest an alternate weight reduction diet for you, similar to a diminished calorie diet, to oversee diabetes. Those with epilepsy should likewise counsel their primary care physician before utilizing this as a feature of their treatment plan.

Does the Ketogenic Diet Work for Type 2 Diabetes?

The keto diet may likewise assist with working on short- and long haul insight among individuals living with

Alzheimer's illness and are encountering gentle intellectual hindrance, as per an efficient survey of randomized controlled preliminaries distributed in Advances in Nourishment in June 2020.

Specialists alert that further examination is expected to affirm these discoveries and demonstrate a circumstance and logical results connection among keto and forestalling dementia.

As far as weight reduction, you might be keen on attempting the ketogenic diet since you've heard that it's anything but a major effect immediately. Also, that might be valid. Ketogenic diets will make you shed pounds inside the principal week. Clarifies that your body will initially go through the entirety of its glycogen stores (the capacity type of starch). With exhausted glycogen, you'll drop water weight. While it tends to be propelling to see the number on the scale go down (regularly drastically), remember that most of this is water misfortune at first.

In any case, the keto diet can be a compelling alternative after some time. One audit recommended the keto diet can prod fat misfortune in large individuals when utilized for a long time and as long as one year.

A meta-investigation noticed that one probably justification for weight reduction is that keto diets may stifle hunger.

One drawback to the ketogenic diet for weight reduction is that it's hard to keep up with. Studies show that weight reduction comes about because being on a low-carb diet for over a year will, in general, be equivalent to being on a typical, solid eating routine. While you might be eating additional satisfying fats (like peanut butter, ordinary spread, or avocado), you're likewise far more restricted in what's permitted on the eating routine, which can make ordinary circumstances, such as dining with family or going out with companions, undeniably more troublesome. Since individuals regularly think that it's extreme to support, it's not difficult to depend on it as a momentary eating regimen instead of a drawn-out way of life.

Another common disadvantage to the keto diet: the keto influenza. One investigation, distributed in Walk 2020 in Outskirts in Sustenance,

discovered that across 43 distinct online discussions for individuals following a keto diet, about 33% of analysts detailed encountering this present moment keto incidental effect. In the initial few days after you start your keto diet plan, you may encounter migraines, muscle cramps, weariness, sickness, clogging, and other influenza-like manifestations, as per Harvard Wellbeing Distributing.

These side effects typically resolve within a couple of days to half a month, and you can assist with countering them by drinking a lot of liquids with electrolytes, as indicated by an article distributed June 2020 in StatPearls.

Before beginning, ask yourself what is truly sensible for you. Then, at that point, get your PCP's alright. You may likewise work with a neighbourhood enrolled dietitian nutritionist to restrict possible supplement inadequacies and talk about nutrient supplementation, as you will not be eating entire grains, dairy, or organic products and will kill numerous veggies. An eating regimen that dispenses with whole nutritional categories is a warning to me. This isn't something to mess with or plunge into carelessly with no clinical management.

What to Remember When Making Your Ketogenic Supper Plan

If you've chosen to push ahead in attempting the keto diet, you will need to adhere to the boundaries of the eating plan. Around 60 to 80 per cent of your calories will come from fats. That implies you'll eat meats, fats, and oils and an extremely restricted measure of nonstarchy vegetables, she says. (This is not quite the same as a conventional low-carb diet, as much fewer carbs are permitted on the keto diet.)

The excess calories in the keto diet come from protein — around 1 gram (g) per kilogram of body weight, so that a 140-pound lady would require around 64 g of protein absolute. Concerning carbs: Each body is unique, yet many people keep up with ketosis with somewhere in the range of 20 and 50 g of net carbs each day. Total carbs short fibre rises to net carbs, she clarifies.

One thing to recollect: It's not difficult to get 'kicked out of ketosis. This means, on the off chance that you eat something as little as a serving of blueberries, your body could return to consuming starches for fuel as opposed to fat.

CHAPTER ONE
A Total Food Manual for Follow

Considering what finds a way into a keto diet — and what doesn't? Know what food sources you'll eat before you start, and how to join more fats into your eating routine,

Protein

Generously Ketogenic eats fewer carbs aren't high in protein (they centre around fat), so these should all be burned-through with some restraint.

• Grass-took care of meat

• Fish, particularly greasy fish, similar to salmon

• Dark meat chicken

Sometimes

• Bacon

• Low-fat proteins, like skinless chicken bosom and shrimp. These are extraordinary to remember for your keto diet, yet add a sauce on top for some fat instead of eating them plain.

Never

• Cold cuts with added sugar (read the mark!)

• Meat that has been marinated in sweet sauces

• Fish or chicken tenders

Oil and Fat

Generously

• Avocado oil

• Olive oil

• Coconut oil

• Butter

• Heavy cream

Sporadically Cutoff your utilization of these oils, which ought to be not difficult to do in case you're staying away from bundled food sources, where they're frequently found.

• Sunflower oil

• Safflower oil

• Corn oil

Never

• Margarine

• Artificial trans fats

Products of the soil

Generously

• Avocado

• Leafy greens, similar to spinach and arugula

• Celery

• Asparagus

Infrequently These are extraordinary decisions; however, you'll have to check the carbs.

• Leeks

• Spaghetti squash

• Eggplant

Never

• Potatoes

• Corn

• Raisins

Nuts and Seeds

Generously

• Walnuts

• Almonds

• Flaxseed and chia seeds

Infrequently

• Unsweetened nut spreads (almond or peanut butter)

• Cashews

• Pistachios

Never

• Trail blends in with a dried organic product

• Sweetened nut or seed margarine

• Chocolate-covered nuts

Dairy Items

Generously

• Cheddar cheddar

• Blue cheddar

• Feta cheddar

Sporadically

• Full-fat curds

• Full-fat plain Greek yoghurt

• Full-fat ricotta cheddar

Never

• Milk

• Sweetened nonfat yoghurt

• Ice cream

Sugars

Generously None; consistently practice balance with sugars.

Sporadically

• Stevia

• Erythritol

• Xylitol

Never

• Agave

• Honey

• Maple syrup

• White and earthy coloured sugars

Toppings and Sauces

Generously

• Guacamole

• Lemon spread sauce

• Mayonnaise (guarantee there's no sugar added)

Every so often

• Raw garlic

• Tomato sauce (search for those with no added sugar)

• Balsamic vinegar

Never

• Barbecue sauce

• Ketchup

• Honey mustard

Beverages

Generously

• Water

• Almond milk

• Bone stock

• Plain tea

Every so often

• Black espresso (watch caffeine utilization)

• Unsweetened carbonated water (limit just if bubbles make you swelled)

• Diet pop

• Zero-calorie drinks

Never

• Soda

• Fruit juice

• Lemonade

Spices and Flavors

Generously All spices and flavours fit in a keto diet; however, in case you're utilizing enormous sums, Mancinelli suggests checking the carbs.

• Salt (salt food varieties to taste)

• Pepper

• Thyme, oregano, paprika, and cayenne

Every so often, These are good decisions yet contain some carbs.

• ground ginger

• Garlic powder

• Onion powder

Never

• No spices and flavours are forbidden; they're by and large alright to use in limited quantities to add flavour to food varieties.

Enhancements

Think about taking

• Fiber

• Multivitamin

Discretionary These assist you to produce ketones more.

CHAPTER TWO

A Nitty-gritty Ketogenic Diet Food Rundown to Follow

Next are the absolute best food varieties to eat on the keto diet, alongside their serving sizes and clarification of why they're useful for individuals who follow this eating approach.

Avocado Oil

Per 1 tablespoon (tbsp) serving 124 calories, 0g net carbs, 0g protein, 14g fat

Advantages This is a decent wellspring of heart-solid monounsaturated unsaturated fats.

Canola Oil

Per 1 tbsp serving 124 calories, 0g net carbs, 0g protein, 14g fat

Advantages Exploration has shown that utilization of canola oil can lessen aggregate and awful cholesterol.

Coconut Oil

Per 1 tbsp serving 116 calories, 0g net carbs, 0g protein, 14g fat

Advantages While high in immersed fat, coconut oil may expand "great" HDL cholesterol levels.

MCT Oil

Per 1 tbsp serving 115 calories, 0g net carbs, 0g protein, 14g fat

Advantages Got from coconut, MCT represents medium-chain fatty substances. Restricted examination proposes MCT oil may help in weight reduction and assist with advancing ketosis.

Margarine

Per 1 tbsp serving 100 calories, 0g net carbs, 0g protein, 11g fat

Advantages, however, the serving gives 11 g of saturated fat; research has discovered that spread is certainly not the main consideration in expanding the hazard of persistent conditions like coronary illness or diabetes.

Cheddar

Per 1 cut serving 113 calories, 0g net carbs, 7g protein, 9g fat

Advantages Cheddar is permitted however you see fit; cheddar is a simple illustration of its nourishment details. One investigation found that cheddar eaters had a 12 per cent lower hazard of type 2 diabetes.

Substantial Cream

Per 1 tbsp serving 52 calories, 0g net carbs, 0g protein, 5g fat

Advantages This is a simple method to add calories and fat into a ketogenic diet.

Bacon

Per 1 cut serving 43 calories, 0g net carbs, 3g protein, 3g fat

Advantages The go-ahead on bacon might be one explanation you're ready for adhering to the eating regimen, as it can make eating events seriously tempting. Watch the sodium content, as it can add up rapidly.

Chicken Thigh

Per 1 thigh serving 318 calories, 0g net carbs, 32g protein, 20g fat

Advantages Leave the skin on here for additional fat. One thigh is a decent wellspring of selenium, zinc, and B nutrients.

Eggs

Per 1 egg serving 77 calories, 1g net carbs, 6g protein, 5g fat

Advantages Eggs contain the ideal team of satisfying protein and fat; they're additionally high in the cancer prevention agent mineral selenium.

Ground Hamburger

Per 3-ounce (oz) serving (estimated crude) 279 calories, 0g net carbs, 12g protein, 24g fat

Advantages Ground hamburger (made with 70% lean meat and 30 per cent fat) is a higher-fat decision — yet that is the point. You'll likewise get a superb wellspring of nutrient B12, which is important to keep up your energy levels.

New York Strip Steak

Per 3 oz serving 224 calories, 0g net carbs, 22g protein, 14g fat

Advantages You'll get an amazing measure of muscle-building protein in addition to satisfying fat in this choice. It's likewise plentiful in zinc, a mineral that advances legitimate thyroid capacity.

Asparagus

Per 1 cup (crude) serving 27 calories, 2g net carbs, 3g protein, 0g fat

Advantages Asparagus contains bone-building calcium and different minerals, like potassium and magnesium, which has been connected with glucose guideline.

Avocado

Per ½ avocado serving 160 calories, 2g net carbs, 2g protein, 15g fat

Advantages The velvety organic products are loaded with fibre, which you may need on the keto diet. They additionally are a phenomenal wellspring of invulnerable firing up nutrient C.

Bok Choy

Per 1 cup (destroyed) serving nine calories, 1g net carbs, 1g protein, 0g fat

Advantages Chinese cabbage is a rich wellspring of nutrients An and C and offers some calcium and energy-boosting iron.

Cauliflower

Per 1 cup (crude) serving 25 calories, 2g net carbs, 2g protein, 0g fat

Advantages Give more than 3/4 of your nutrient C amount in a day; with 3 g of fibre, it's likewise a decent wellspring of the heart-sound supplement.

Celery

Per 1 cup (crude) serving 16 calories, 1g net carbs, 1g protein, 0g fat

Advantages Celery is perhaps the most hydrating veggie out there. These crunchy skewers additionally contain nutrients A and K and folate.

Cucumber

Per ½ cup (cuts) serving eight calories, 2g net carbs, 0g protein, 0g fat

Advantages Cukes are high in water, settling on them a hydrating decision. They're additionally a shockingly decent wellspring of nutrient K, a nutrient significant for legitimate blood coagulating and bone development.

Green Peppers

Per 1 cup (cut) serving 18 calories, 2g net carbs, 1g protein, 0g fat

Advantages Alongside over a day's prerequisites for nutrient C, they're additionally a decent wellspring of nutrient B6, which assumes a part over 100 chemical responses in the body.

Lettuce

Per 1 cup (destroyed) serving five calories, 1g net carbs, 0g protein, 0g fat

Advantages Mixed greens can add mass to your dinners for not many calories, just as skin-fortifying nutrient An and nutrient C.

Mushrooms

Per 1 cup (crude) serving 15 calories, 1g net carbs, 2g protein, 0g fat

Advantages Mushrooms are known for their potential resistant boosting properties, as one investigation recommended.

They're additionally a superb wellspring of B nutrients.

Zucchini

Per 1 cup (cut, crude) serving 18 calories, 3g net carbs, 1g protein, 0g fat

Advantages This is an extraordinary method to sneak in extra fibre, and the veggie likewise offers a decent wellspring of manganese. This mineral assists structure with boning and helps in glucose control.

CHAPTER THREE

7-Day Test Menu for the Keto Diet

Day 1

Breakfast Fried eggs in margarine on a bed of lettuce finished off with avocado.

Nibble Sunflower seeds

Lunch Spinach salad with barbecued salmon

Nibble Celery and pepper strips plunged in guacamole.

Supper Pork slash with cauliflower crush and red cabbage slaw

Day 2

Breakfast Impenetrable espresso (made with spread and coconut oil), hard-bubbled eggs

Nibble Macadamia nuts

Lunch Fish salad stuffed in tomatoes.

Bite Cook meat and cut cheddar roll-ups

Supper Meatballs on zucchini noodles finished off with cream sauce.

Day 3

Breakfast Cheddar and veggie omelette finished off with salsa.

Nibble Plain, full-fat Greek yoghurt finished off with squashed walnuts.

Lunch Sashimi takeout with miso soup

Nibble Smoothie made with almond milk, greens, almond spread, and protein powder.

Supper Simmered chicken with asparagus and sautéed mushrooms

Day 4

Breakfast Smoothie made with almond milk, greens, almond margarine, and protein powder.

Nibble Two hard-bubbled eggs

Lunch Chicken strips made with almond flour on a bed of greens with cucumbers and goat cheddar

Bite Cut cheddar and ringer pepper cuts

Supper Barbecued shrimp finished off with a lemon spread sauce with a side of asparagus.

Day 5

Breakfast Seared eggs with bacon and a side of greens

Nibble A small bunch of pecans with a quarter cup of berries

Lunch Grass-took care of burger in a lettuce "bun" finished off with avocado and a side plate of mixed greens.

Nibble Celery sticks plunged in the almond spread.

Supper Prepared tofu with cauliflower rice, broccoli, and peppers, finished off with a handcrafted nut sauce.

Day 6

Breakfast Prepared eggs in avocado cups

Nibble Kale chips

Lunch Poached salmon avocado rolls enveloped by ocean growth (sans rice)

Nibble Meat-based bar (turkey or pork)

Supper Barbecued hamburger kebabs with peppers and sautéed broccolini

Day 7

Breakfast Eggs mixed with veggies finished off with salsa.

Tidbit Dried ocean growth strips and cheddar

Lunch Sardine salad made with mayo into equal parts an avocado.

Nibble Turkey jerky (search for no added sugars)

Supper Cooked trout with margarine, sautéed bok choy

CHAPTER FOUR
20 Keto Diet Dinners You Can Make Early

Are you hoping to stir up your keto feast plan? Here's a gathering of low-carb plans you can prepare once and partake in the entire week.

Zucchini noodles are a keto-accommodating side dish alternative that is a snap to whip up!

If you live someplace that carbs are in pretty much everything, adhering to a strict food routine like the keto diet can feel incomprehensible.

One of the ketogenic diet challenges, an incredibly low-carb diet that utilizes fat for fuel rather than sugars, is how prohibitive it is. To keep your body in a condition of ketosis, simply 5 to 10 per cent of calories can emerge out of carbs. At the same time, 75% or higher should come from fat (and any excess calories from protein), as indicated by the Harvard T.H. Chan School of General Wellbeing. In any case, when you cut out carbs, a macronutrient that keeps our bodies sustained and working, finding keto-accommodating food sources can be a big test,

One inadequately picked dinner can kick you off ketosis. Particularly when you're initially beginning, get ready suppers ahead of time, so you're following the eating regimen precisely to remain in ketosis. Ketosis is the metabolic state key to some low-carb abstains from food, including keto; it triggers the consumption of carbs rather than fat for fuel, an investigation notes.

Keeping in ketosis is only one explanation feast arranging is imperative to keeping up with the high-fat, low-carb diet. Removing carbs significantly shrivels the rundown of food sources you're ready to eat, making it that a lot simpler for you to become supplement lacking. To keep away from this, fusing a lot of nonstarchy vegetables into your eating regimen to guarantee that you're getting sufficient fibre and pivot protein sources to incorporate things like fish, so you're not continually eating red meat or poultry.

Besides being denied of supplements it's familiar with getting, your body likewise isn't accustomed to being in ketosis. The unexpected change to this metabolic state can prompt what's known as the keto influenza, which can torment you with flulike indications that can go from cerebral pains, shortcoming, and touchiness to stoppage, nausea, and spewing.

This is a routine that is hard to stay with — there are more adjusted methods of getting thinner. Likewise, the keto diet doesn't underline sound fats, and food sources high in soaked fat, similar to cheddar and margarine, can build the danger of coronary illness.

Albeit numerous specialists shun the keto diet, if it's done cautiously and effectively, it might prompt fast (but regularly transitory) weight reduction, and it might assist with balancing out your glucose in case you're overseeing type 2 diabetes, noticed an article distributed in Walk 2019 in StatPearls.

A few examinations, similar to a 50-member study distributed in July 2016 in the diary Epilepsy and Conduct, have shown that the keto diet can lessen seizures in kids with epilepsy. In any case, late surveys — like one distributed in 2019 in the diary Wildernesses in Neuroscience — reason that the absence of excellent investigations implies that more exploration should be led to distinguish the components of activity that lead to positive outcomes for kids with epilepsy.

The keto diet isn't for everybody, and now and again, it can be risky to your wellbeing. Those in danger for coronary illness should look to different choices to get more fit, and she instructs anybody with a set of experiences regarding a dietary issue (that incorporates voraciously consuming food problem) to keep away from any craze diet as it might exasperate side effects or bring back unfortunate eating practices.

If you're focused on attempting keto, consistently talk with an enlisted dietitian to study the eating routine and get help making a dinner plan. To try not to eat bacon and fat bombs each day, we gathered together 20 fast and straightforward keto-accommodating top choices you can make early.

1. Keto Bison Chicken Hacked Salad

Bacon? Blue cheddar? Bison sauce? Say no more. This super plate of mixed greens is pressed with supplements and requires just around 20 minutes to prepare early. With 17.2 grams (g) of carbs (yet 8.7 g net carbs) and 46.4 g fat, this plate of mixed greens likewise gets you fibre, potassium, and protein. While not perceived by an authority logical body like the Foundation of Sustenance and Dietetics or the Workplace of Infection Counteraction and Wellbeing Advancement, Net carbs are total carbs short fibre and sugar alcohols, per Atkins.com. Some keto weight watchers check these rather than total carbs because it recommends how much food may spike your glucose. However, remember this is the best guess. Numerous variables, including how handled something is, can influence how much food may affect glucose. Short version, think about a food's net carb sum while considering other factors. For this formula specifically, be aware of what brand of sauce you use — numerous prepackaged sauces contain added sugars.

2. Keto Dinner Prep Breakfast Bombs

Breakfast can be challenging to prepare for on the keto diet. However, these morning meal bombs are not difficult to make early and freeze well. This quick breakfast nibble has recently 4.7 g total carbs, 2.7 g net carbs, and 24.6 g fat. To fulfil all your taste buds, showering on some sans sugar maple syrup indeed draws out the spice of the bacon.

3. Cauliflower Hummus With Harissa Wafers

At the point when you're on a prohibitive eating regimen like keto, making up for your carb-moulded shortfall with snacks is an unquestionable requirement. Since chickpeas and different vegetables are high in carbs, hummus is typically a no-no. Be that as it may, this cauliflower hummus work-around is comparably scrumptious and meets the keto measures with 18.33 g total carbs and 4.96 g net carbs. To give the cauliflower an additional kick, pair it with these simple-to-make harissa wafers likewise remembered for the formula.

4. Keto Messy Joe Skillet Supper

This supper dish is rich, delicious, thus loaded with flavour you wouldn't have a clue about; it's a keto formula. Extraordinary for clump cooking, this formula requires just a tiny bunch of fixings found around the house, and it has 6.8 g carbs and 5.1 g net carbs. You can heap your sloppy joe on a low-carb bun or into lettuce cups for an additional crunch or serve on top of squashed cauliflower.

5. Sweet Stew Keto Pork Slashes

Speedy to cook and high in fat, pork slashes are an extraordinary protein elective for weeknight meals — and make for incredible lunch extras, as well. This formula calls for skillet burning the pork cleaves, then, at that point, spooning on a habit-forming sweet stew sauce. With just 3 g net carbs (counting the sauce), you can balance this dish with a side of zucchini noodles or cauliflower rice. (This blog doesn't list them all out carbs for this formula.)

6. Simple Keto Swedish Meatballs

On the off chance that you've at any point been charmed by the Swedish meatballs at Ikea, presently, you can make your form at home — and indeed, they're keto-accommodating. A family most loved that you can have prepared shortly or less, these meatballs are slathered in a smooth sauce and pair consummately with pounded cauliflower. Furthermore, don't avoid the salt; the sodium in the meatballs can help keep up your electrolytes to battle indications of keto influenza. Takes note of the Harvard T.H. Chan School of General Wellbeing. Three meatballs clock 1 g all out carbs, making this a genuinely keto-accommodating food.

7. Low-Carb Blackberry-Filled Lemon Almond-Flour Biscuits

Biscuits are an American staple for in and out morning meals, yet they're regularly loaded with carbs and added sugar. Made with almond flour, these without grain biscuits have a tart blackberry loading up with a bit of lemon. These biscuits freeze well, so they are extraordinary to make in clumps, and everyone has just 4 g all out carbs and 1 g net carbs.

8. Nut Ginger Cold Noodle Salad

Dinner prep is much simpler when you don't need to cook. Ideal for snacks and hot days when you fear turning on the oven, this ginger vegetarian noodle salad requires just five minutes to make and has 7.5 g net carbs per serving. (This blog doesn't indicate the total carbs per serving.) You can trade out peanut butter for almond or sunflower seed margarine and use coconut aminos rather than tamari on the off chance you need to go without soy.

9. Zucchini Noodles With Avocado Shrimp Pesto

However, if you love shrimp, you have been quitting because they're so low in fat, and avocado can tackle that issue. Prepared in under 20 minutes, this new, lively dish is ideal for snacks and fast meals. It has 47 g all out carbs in two servings, coming out to 18 g net carbs per serving.

10. Cream of Asparagus Soup

This without dairy soup utilizes coconut milk to make a rich, smooth base and makes in clumps. With 5.2 g carbs and 3.7 g net carbs, this light soup additionally offers fibre. Partake in your bowl, hot or cold. Sprinkle disintegrated bacon on top for a touch of crunch.

11. Keto Johnnycake

Grains like corn and quinoa are generally no-nos on the keto diet because of their high carb content. However, fortunately, this "hoecake" formula is really without corn. This keto corncake substitute is cosy, with only a little sweet, requiring negligible fixings like almond flour and powdered sugar. This dish has 3.5 g total carbs (and just 1.5 g net carbs) and functions admirably as a side to sop up sassy meat dishes, similar to ribs or pulled pork, or as a speedy in and out breakfast nibble.

12. Slashed Mediterranean Serving of mixed greens With Sun-Dried Tomato Vinaigrette

Mixed greens are one of the most effortless (and when arranged well, best) things to make early when you're on a high-fat, low-carb diet. Layered with a tart sun-dried tomato dressing, one serving of this plate of mixed greens gets both of you servings of vegetables. This formula has 9 g carbs and 7 g net carbs per serving; however, if you're searching for a lower carb tally, add some lettuce to build it up.

13. Keto Strawberry Fudge Pops

At the point when you're on a careful nutritional plan as prohibitive as keto, you have the right to enjoy without having to continually stress over being kicked out of ketosis. These fudgy strawberry pops make a reviving daytime nibble or after-dinner treat, and they can also be made with blackberries, blueberries, or raspberries. Ensure you're utilizing dim chocolate with around 70% cocoa for it to be keto-accommodating. One pop will hinder you from just 4 g carbs and 3 g net carbs.

14. Keto Taco Cheeseburgers

This formula consolidates the most innovative possible solution: tacos and burgers. These burgers are speedy and straightforward to make, with minor kitchen cleanup required for a unique barbecuing formula for summer. Present with blended greens or a low-carb bun, or appreciate as a lettuce wrap. You can dive into one of these burgers effortlessly, realizing that you're devouring a simple 2.3 g carbs and 1.6 g net carbs.

15. Keto Spread Chicken

If you're threatened by making Indian food, this simple spread chicken formula is the ideal spot to begin. With 6.25 g carbs and 6 g net carbs, this decadent dish can be made with chicken, sheep, hamburger, or even veggies if you're hoping to pack in more fibre. Balance this supper with cauliflower rice or low-carb naan bread for a beautiful weeknight supper — it additionally makes incredible extras for lunch.

16. Chicken and Arugula Salad with Watermelon

Leafy foods don't generally blend, yet on account of chicken and watermelon, it works. This formula is a go-to if you don't have the opportunity to cook, and it tends to be an extraordinary method to go through any extra chicken. Peppery yet invigorating, this serving of mixed greens is brimming with nutritious fixings, in addition to pecans, avocado, olive oil, and feta cheddar to up the fat substance. This blog doesn't list the macros in question. However, you can have confidence that the fixings are all keto-accommodating.

17. Spinach and Salmon Burgers

It very well may be challenging to design family-accommodating suppers on the keto diet. However, these fresh salmon burgers will keep everybody glad and hungry for additional. This burger is a keto-weight watcher's fantasy with just 6.2 g all out carbs (and a simple 0.3 g net carbs). Finished off with fragrant dill and natively constructed mayo, this burger can be eaten all alone or presented with low-carb keto flatbread.

18. Custom made Protein Bars

Protein bars are, as a rule, untouchable on keto due to the high carb and protein content — in addition, in the same way as other handled food varieties, they can be costly and aren't the best decisions. Yet, protein bars can likewise be a good and filling nibble for individuals who are continually in a hurry or again if you're having a nibble-related crisis. You can make these natively constructed bars with macadamia dinner or destroyed coconut and inject them with matcha powder, dim chocolate, or cinnamon. This formula doesn't list the nourishment realities. However, the fixings included all fit in a keto diet.

19. Keto Pizza Bagels

If you're simply beginning keto and thinking about how you will get by without your morning bagel, don't surrender. Made with almond flour and cheddar, this pizza bagel formula takes under 30 minutes to make and has 10 g carbs and 6 g net carbs per bagel. You can likewise make the mixture in enormous groups and stick to utilize later for keto pizza, keto pretzels, or keto empanadas. Yum!

20. Mushroom Cauliflower Risotto

This dish will not pass as customary in Italy, yet it will fulfil any risotto desires for those on the keto diet. This formula has fundamentally similar overall fixings; you need to trade out ordinary rice for cauliflower rice. With 7.7 g carbs and 5.1 g net carbs, this sets impeccably with a burned steak or makes a shockingly decent breakfast presented for sure eggs.

Fast to cook and high in fat, pork hacks are an incredible protein elective for weeknight meals — and make for great lunch extras, as well. This formula calls for container singing the pork cleaves, then, at that point, spooning on a habit-forming sweet bean stew sauce. With just 3 g net carbs (counting the sauce), you can balance this dish with a side of zucchini noodles or cauliflower rice. (This blog doesn't list the total carbs for this formula.)

CHAPTER FIVE
CONCLUSION

The Ketogenic diet is perhaps the best eating routine you can follow for weight reduction and improve your general wellbeing. The eating routine can likewise be utilized for youngsters who are overweight. Various examinations help the eating regimen showing critical outcomes, particularly when combined with exe. High carb and high protein eating will bring about an abundance of muscle versus fat because of the sugar content in these supplements. So excessive eating of any supplement is unfortunate and causes weight to acquire. However, a sound eating routine comprises an equilibrium of protein, carbs and fats as indicated by the resistance levels of your body. Pretty much everybody can achieve a ketogenic diet with sufficient persistence and exertion. Also, we can direct various real conditions normally with keto. Insulin opposition raised glucose, aggravation, corpulence, type-2 diabetes are some ailments that keto can assist with settling. These undesirable conditions will lessen and standardize for the casualty who follows a sound ketogenic diet. Low-carb, high-fat and moderate protein entire food sources give the extraordinary medical advantages of this eating regimen.